theatre & mind

Bruce McConachie

palgrave
macmillan

First published 2013 by
PALGRAVE MACMILLAN

Palgrave Macmillan in the UK is an imprint of Macmillan
Publishers Limited, registered in England, company number
785998, of Houndmills, Basingstoke, Hampshire RG21 6XS.

Palgrave Macmillan in the US is a division of St Martin's Press LLC,
175 Fifth Avenue, New York, NY 10010.

Palgrave Macmillan is the global academic imprint of the above
companies and has companies and representatives throughout
the world.

Palgrave® and Macmillan® are registered trademarks in the United
States, the United Kingdom, Europe and other countries

ISBN: 978–0–230–27583–6 paperback

This book is printed on paper suitable for recycling and made
from fully managed and sustained forest sources. Logging,
pulping and manufacturing processes are expected to conform to
the environmental regulations of the country of origin.

A catalogue record for this book is available from the British Library.

Library of Congress Cataloging-in-Publication Data

McConachie, Bruce A.
    Theatre and mind / Bruce McConachie.
        p. cm.—(Theatre&)
    Includes index.
    ISBN 978–0–230–27583–6
        1. Acting – Psychological aspects. 2. Actors – Psychology.
    3. Theater audiences – Psychology. 4. Theater – Semiotics. I. Title.

PN2071.P78M385 2013
792.01—dc23   2012032290

10 9 8 7 6 5 4 3 2 1
22 21 20 19 18 17 16 15 14 13

Printed in China

contents

series editors' preface

The theatre is everywhere, from entertainment districts to the fringes, from the rituals of government to the ceremony of the courtroom, from the spectacle of the sporting arena to the theatres of war. Across these many forms stretches a theatrical continuum through which cultures both assert and question themselves.

Theatre has been around for thousands of years, and the ways we study it have changed decisively. It's no longer enough to limit our attention to the canon of Western dramatic literature. Theatre has taken its place within a broad spectrum of performance, connecting it with the wider forces of ritual and revolt that thread through so many spheres of human culture. In turn, this has helped make connections across disciplines; over the past fifty years, theatre and performance have been deployed as key metaphors and practices with which to rethink gender, economics, war, language, the fine arts, culture and one's sense of self.

Theatre & is a long series of short books which hopes to capture the restless interdisciplinary energy of theatre and performance. Each book explores connections between theatre and some aspect of the wider world, asking how the theatre might illuminate the world and how the world might illuminate the theatre. Each book is written by a leading theatre scholar and represents the cutting edge of critical thinking in the discipline.

We have been mindful, however, that the philosophical and theoretical complexity of much contemporary academic writing can act as a barrier to a wider readership. A key aim for these books is that they should all be readable in one sitting by anyone with a curiosity about the subject. The books are challenging, pugnacious, visionary sometimes and, above all, clear. We hope you enjoy them.

Jen Harvie and Dan Rebellato

theatre & mind

Introduction

Picking a good title for a book can be a difficult decision. The 'Theatre &' series simplifies the process by limiting the choice to a single appropriate noun that will follow the ampersand to complete the title for each book. That's fine for a book that will focus on politics, audiences, or ethics – some of the topics (and part of the titles) featured in this series. I chose 'mind' for my follow-the-ampersand noun because it is the most appropriate choice for a book centered on the cognitive operations that underlie and constitute theatrical participation for human beings. But 'Theatre & Mind' is also misleading in two important respects. First, the title isolates the mind as a separate entity, suggesting a Cartesian division between brain and body, thinking and feeling. In fact, this short book will demonstrate the opposite proposition: The mind is embodied. Not only must the mind work within a living body, but the ways we think – our sense of

1

self and the foundational concepts we use to perceive the world and other people in it – derive from the embeddedness of our bodies on planet earth. Our minds do not float above the messiness of material reality.

Further, thinking cannot occur without emotional involvement. The chemistry of emotions first occurs in our brains, and all cognitive scientists now recognize that emotion cannot be divided from even the most abstract of thoughts. In this regard, it's nice to see that science has caught up with the theatre. Theatre artists and scholars have known all along that thinking and feeling are intimately intertwined. Some cognitive scientists and acting teachers have suggested that the term 'bodymind' should be adopted to indicate how cognition really works. Titling this book *Theatre & Bodymind*, however, would likely have created more confusion than interest and anticipation.

The second problem with the chosen title is that 'mind' is a noun and not a verb. This is a difficulty because cognition is best characterized as an active process, not as an object or a state of being. Our minds are continuously interacting with our immediate surroundings, as well as with memories from the past and expectations about the future. Cognitive scientists have abandoned the older idea of a mind essentially empty at birth, waiting to be filled by personal experiences, family relationships, and historical cultures that shape who we are and how we interact with others. The idea of the mind as a blank slate, which derives from Enlightenment philosopher John Locke, is no longer tenable. As we will see in the following pages, the mind is primed to be pro-active even before birth, constructing perceptions and motivating actions rather than passively recording what happens to us. Family and culture still matter, of course, but scientists now understand that nature is as important as nurture in cognitive processing; our genetic inheritance and the early experiences of infancy are crucial in shaping our cognitive re-working of the world.

Like embodiment, the notion of the mind as interactive has been a part of our sense of theatre for a long time. We know how important interactions among performers can be for sparking dramatic interest on stage. We prize actor–audience interaction as a significant part of live theatre. And we recognize that the kinds of emotional interactions among spectators that generate raucous laughter or awed silence help to constitute some of our best memories in the theatre. Nonetheless, 'minding', to move the noun of the title into a verbal form, is not a real option for entitling this book. *Theatre & Minding* would connote paying attention and obeying orders – 'mind the gap' – rather than enjoying the interactions of good theatre. Despite its shortcomings regarding embodiedness and interactivity, *Theatre & Mind* will have to do as a title.

As this discussion suggests, *Theatre & Mind* seeks to plunge the reader into the cognitive depths of theatre itself. All performance depends upon our species-wide abilities to create, perceive, emote, remember, imagine, and empa-thize – cognitive operations that have come under new scrutiny in the past thirty years from scientists in psychology, linguistics, neuroscience, and other fields. Further, these cognitive operations are not specific to the theatre; there is no discrete part of the mind dedicated solely to creating and enjoying performances. When people participate in theatrical activities, they engage the same kinds of cognitive fundamentals that they use to drive a car, carry on a conversation, and solve a problem in mathematics. Theatre artists and scholars have known in a commonsense way about some of these fundamentals for many years. But cognitive scientists have discovered many aspects of memory, perception, empathy, and the other cognitive foundations of performance that theatre scholars are only beginning to incorporate into their understanding of the art form. In addition, several of the experimentally based conclusions of cognitive science undermine assumptions and ideas about performing and spectating that most theatre artists, critics, and historians take for granted.

Other social scientific and humanistic disciplines allied with theatre and performance studies have been incorporating the findings of cognitive science for more than a decade. In anthropology and philosophy, for example, scholars are using ideas from the cognitive sciences to ask new questions about religious rituals and the limits of objective knowledge. Musicologists are working closely with cognitive scientists to explore the many connections between music and emotion. Scholars in film studies and literature are relying on tested insights about our minds to investigate how people can put together and make meaning from stories told on film or through words on a page. All of these endeavors have obvious relevance for theatre and performance studies; we could use some scientific grounding for our assertions about rituals, emotions, and narratives. Further, like all of the sciences, the cognitive sciences rest on falsifiability. That is, only truth claims that can be potentially falsified through empirical tests and logical reasoning are allowed to stand as provisional insights. Our discipline came late to the inter-disciplinary conversations in cognitive studies, however. Only in the past five years have a few books been published that attempt to understand the theatre from the perspective of cognitive science. I have drawn on them for this study and list them in the further reading.

One of the major reasons for our tardiness is that most scholars in our discipline remain committed to one or another area of poststructuralist theory, an orientation to knowledge that does not recognize the value of empirical science for humanistic investigation. Partly because post-structuralism inherited a blank-slate understanding of mind and society, most poststructuralists believe that human perceptions about gender roles, class relations, historical causality, and similar phenomena are entirely socially con-structed and have nothing to do with evolution and biology. Poststructuralists also believe in epistemological relativism. Because truth claims can never be entirely disentangled from ideology, they hold that all knowledge is subjective and relative. In contrast, although few scientists claim absolute objectivity for their findings, most do believe that testable explanations concerning the material world are better than ones that cannot be tested. Until we get a better explanation for why objects thrown up in the air fall toward the earth, for example, scientists are willing to accept what physicists currently understand as the law of gravity. Because of their objections to science, poststructuralists do not subject their insights to empirical investigation; the propositions of poststructuralist theorists such as Michel Foucault, Jacques Lacan, and Jacques Derrida are not falsifiable. As a result of poststructuralist antipathy to science, few theatre and performance scholars have bothered to learn anything about breakthroughs in the cognitive sciences that might challenge their assumptions about what theatre is and how it works.

I have addressed these and other problems with poststructuralism in *Engaging Audiences: A Cognitive Approach to Spectating in the Theatre* (2008) and will not elaborate them here. Besides, my goal and my anticipated readership for *Theatre & Mind* are very different.

Instead, I hope that this book will provide a brief introduction for students to the cognitive foundations of theatre studies. In this regard, I rejoice that the 'Theatre &' series is aimed primarily at undergraduate students. As a teacher, I have found that bright undergrads are often eager to discover how their classes in biology, psychology, and other sciences might inform what they can know about creating and understanding theatre and performance. While *Theatre & Mind* is not a practical guide with formulas and exercises ready-made for immediate application, students will be able to connect its insights to their own activities of acting in, viewing, and writing about performances.

In encouraging you to adopt ideas from the cognitive sciences to enable your work in the theatre, I do not mean to suggest that I will throw you into a maze of mind-numbing scientific protocol and terminology. To the extent possible, I will simplify the science and focus on its implications for theatrical study and artistry. I will also limit the kind of scientific knowledge presented in this book. The rapid expansion of the cognitive sciences in the past thirty years has produced several competing schools of thought among scientists in all of the major areas of research. This is not to say that cognitive science is a wildly speculative enterprise; scientists already know a great deal from their empirical experiments, and much of this basic knowledge is unlikely to change. Rather, scientists tend to disagree mostly at the level of interpretive synthesis, where lab results and real-world observations can fit into a variety of intermediate and encompassing theories.

I will rely on cognitive theories that understand the mind as both embodied and interactive. The sciences of cognition have changed substantially since the 1950s, when researchers took the computer as a general model for the brain. An embodied and interactive orientation to cognition also differs radically from the older stimulus–response model of human action, the behaviorist paradigm that predominated in psychology and the social sciences during the middle decades of the twentieth century. Unfortunately, behaviorism also shaped much performance theory during the twentieth century, especially with regard to acting and spectating. Consequently you will find that parts of *Theatre & Mind* raise significant questions about some of the ideas of Bertolt Brecht, Lee Strasberg, and other theatrical artists of the last century.

Scientific experiments have given initial validation to all of the ideas I will be discussing in this book. This does not mean, however, that scientists fully understand the implications of their experiments, nor can I make the claim that I have always correctly understood these implications when explaining what the theatre is and does. Because of the difficulty of controlling for variables in actual theatrical performances, scientists have run few experiments on actors and spectators in the midst of a production. We now have some brain images of people watching film clips inside an fMRI machine, but it is not feasible to replicate all of the conditions of a live performance for similar experiments.

Will the current experiments and theories relating to embodiment and interactivity give us the final word on the cognitive dynamics of theatre? Of course not. Like Godot in Beckett's play, that final word will never arrive. Nobody will ever deliver absolute truth in a book about biology or anthropology, either, but this does not stop research, writing, teaching, and learning in these fields from using the best that recent science has to offer in their introductions for students. With luck, the shelf life of *Theatre & Mind* will be about twenty years. In 2032, another scholar interested in the cognitive basis of theatre should update this book to include new insights from the cognitive sciences and correct the mistakes that I (unknowingly) am fated to make.

Playing

The evolution of play

Perhaps the best approach for beginning to understand the cognitive foundations of theatre is through human evolution. Contemporary cognitive scientists continue to rely on many of the ideas of Charles Darwin, whose *On the Origin of Species* (1859) established natural selection through genetic variation as the primary engine of evolutionary change. In terms of the evolution of the human brain, scientists generally distinguish among three main stages – reptilian, limbic, and neo-cortical. These stages of mental evolution continue to structure the three major areas of the human brain today. We inherited the most primitive functions of our brains, such as the control of breathing, heart rate, and fight-or-flight reflexes, from our reptilian ancestors. On top of the reptilian brain inside of our skulls sits the limbic brain, which regulates attention processing, long-term memory, and most of our emotional lives. Surrounding these two areas, just under the crown of our head, is the neo-cortex. The neo-cortical stage of mental evolution facilitated better memory, conceptual thinking and language, and the mysterious ability that allows us to think about cognition at all, which we call consciousness. As we will see toward the end of this section, the neo-cortex also allows us to do conceptual integration, the mental operation that facilitates theatrical playing. What eventually became the human brain evolved over millions of years, and did not arrive at its present capabilities until roughly 150,000 years ago, when *Homo sapiens* emerged as a unique species. Although the brain continues to evolve through natural selection, the flexibility of our present brains is such that humans are much better at creativity and innovation than other species on the planet.

Of course, human culture (including the theatre) would be impossible without this evolutionary foundation. There is also significant evidence, however, that the cultures of our hominid ancestors helped to alter the later stages of the biological evolution of our species. (Hominids, also called hominins, are the family of primates from which we evolved; our species, *Homo sapiens*, is the only extant species of hominids.) Biology shaped culture, but culture also shaped some parts of our biology. Most scientists now believe that hominid cooperation and communication (even before the emergence of language) gave our ancestors an evolutionary edge in the struggle for survival. That is, those proto-human species that used culture to expand their neo-cortical brains flourished, while others on nearby branches of the evolutionary tree died off. When hominids acquired the ability to pass down their learning to the next generation and those children could build on what their elders had taught them, our ancestors had mastered mental skills that separated them the other higher mammals. Even chimpanzees and bonobos, the closest species to humans in evolutionary terms, cannot teach and learn in complex ways while living in the wild. Teaching, learning, and repeating an activity together – typically with some variation – is the basis of all human cultures. Significantly, it is also a good definition for rehearsing, performing, and running a piece of theatre (or any kind of performance), according to performance studies scholar Richard Schechner. For perhaps four million years of pre-human history, evolution favored small bands of hominids whose cultural activities were helping to expand the capabilities of the neo-cortical brain in the hominid gene pool.

Most importantly for our species, genetics and culture worked together in the activities of play. Although most of the animal kingdom cannot engage in play, higher mammals, some birds, and a few other species have evolved a genetic predisposition for playing together. Mammalian play includes pretend fighting among mice, running and jumping among antelope and other herd animals, and even proto-human versions of follow-the-leader and hide-and-seek among elephants and dolphins. To begin play, animals signal their intent through specific sounds and/or movements that allay a fight-or-flight response. In addition to exercising some conscious intention about playing, animals set play time apart from their other activities, such as eating or hunting. Animals also take pleasure in their mutual play together; the brains of rats, for example, produce chemicals that induce joy while they are playing. Like other higher mammals, humans also exercise some conscious control over their play, frame play as a separate event, and enjoy their play activities. Despite these continuities in the playing of all animals, however, non-human species generally play in repetitive and habitual ways. Animals do not invent new modes of play and cannot play in ways that require following simple rules or adopting new roles (at least not without human help).

There is little doubt that hominid play put evolutionary pressure on the gene pool of our emerging species to develop and enhance the capabilities of our neo-cortical brains. In short, play helped our ancestors to survive and flourish. Scientists have found that the amount and range of play in higher mammals correlate with their general flexibility when faced with a problem of survival. Animals that play together train each other and themselves in social give-and-take and strategies of attack-and-defense. Playing allows animals to refine their physical and mental skills in situations of low danger so that they can fare better when danger pounces. Not only did playing aid our ancestors in these ways, but it also seems to have sharpened the hominid ability to recognize, repeat, and refine patterns. Drawing on scientific conclusions from biology, archaeology, and evolutionary psychology, evolutionary literary critic Brian Boyd emphasizes the importance of pattern making and perceiving in human evolution. Unlike other animals that have been tested, humans perceive patterns in a face or the night sky and take joy in making patterns when they fashion a tool or a performance. Boyd, who is particularly interested in locating the origins of narrative patterns in the evolution of human play, relates patterning to the creation and reception of all art. For Boyd, art is 'a kind of cognitive *play*, the set of activities designed to engage human *attention* through their own appeal to our preference for inferentially rich and therefore *patterned* information' (*On the Origin of*

Stories, 2009, p. 85; italics in original). Boyd's definition includes the theatre; from productions of *Oedipus Rex* to *Twelfth Night* to *Sweeney Todd*, theatre artists have purposefully played with their audiences to create patterns of movement and sound that grab spectator attention.

Of course, primitive kinds of performing began long before our species created written plays and musicals. Boyd, following the work of other evolutionary psychologists, supposes that pre-human, proto-performances probably began about two million years ago and featured chanting, drumming, body decoration, and dancing among bands of hominids. These were likely exuberant and emotional events intended primarily to forge group solidarity in the face of a threatening world. Such early forms of group play also coordinated new skills with old memories, as well as exploring emerging types of pattern and attention. An important part of such collective play among these bands must have involved hominid–environment relationships; our ancestors consciously incorporated into (or excluded from) their play trees, rocks, dwellings, and other parts of their natural and built environments. Those performing their sounds and movements needed places to stand, emote, and dance, while others, temporarily attentive to their patterns, probably looked on from good vantage points before joining in the action. Well before the evolution of language, hominids likely adopted behaviors that would later develop into acting and spectating in environments set aside for performance. Of course, such relationships involving movement and sound within specific environments occurred in all areas of hominid life, not just while they engaged in performance-like play. Like other higher animals, our ancestors developed senses and brains that could perceive their immediate surroundings and spark appropriate action to survive within them.

Cognitive scientist James J. Gibson created what has come to be termed an ecological psychology to explain organism–environment interaction. For Gibson, 'the environment' is not an objective phenomenon defined by chemistry and biology, but the immediate physical surround of an organism, affording it certain possibilities for action and constraining other options. Gibson coined the term 'affordances' to specify what people can do with perceived objects that are near them. Given human anatomy, for example, some objects afford grasping, and some afford throwing, while others can be jumped on or turned into a drum. In terms of current theatrical practice, designers and directors must be aware of potential affordances when they agree on the setting for a production, its props, and even its costumes. How do the objects on stage – that door up left on the set, this revolver on the mantelpiece, that corset on the leading lady – afford or constrain the necessary actions of the play? As in all performances, every environment for human activity is a field of potential affordances. Our hominid ancestors necessarily adapted their playing to the physical affordances of their immediate surroundings.

Evolution, empathy, and emotions

In addition to object–organism interactions, hominid play had to work within organism–organism relations. Empathy was an important early cognitive tool to facilitate social interaction. There is no agreement among cognitive psychologists on a definition of empathy. Most scientists, however, identify empathy as the cognitive operation by which one person can come to know something about what another person is intending and feeling. In this sense, empathy is a kind of mind-reading that allows one person to step into the shoes of another and experience that person's world from her or his point of view. This notion of empathy as perspective-taking differs from the commonplace view that confuses empathy with sympathy. For most cognitive scientists and philosophers, empathy is not an emotion, as sympathy is. The cognitive operation of empathy may lead to a feeling of care and concern, but empathy can also lead to antipathy, the opposite of sympathy. In a typical, old-fashioned melodrama, for example, nineteenth-century spectators first empathized with the villain – they imaginatively put themselves in his shoes to figure out what he was doing – before they decided that he was more worthy of boos and hisses than smiles and sobs.

Biologist and philosopher Evan Thompson notes that different levels of empathy occur over several phases (*Mind in Life*, 2007, pp. 382–401). He terms the first phase 'sensorimotor coupling' and links it to the recent discovery of mirror neurons. Although most of the research on mirror neurons has been done on monkeys and other non-human mammals, there is a growing consensus that humans have mirror neurons that operate in the same or similar ways. In brief, mirror neurons are networks of brain cells in the neo-cortex that 'light up' in response to intentional motor action. Significantly, these networks in your brain respond in the same way whether you perform the action yourself or see someone else do it. Let's say that you are sitting in the audience and watching an actor on stage get angry while performing a character who is trying to dominate another actor/character on stage. As the actor's face and body express this emotion, your mirror neurons for facial and bodily anger will fire in the same way as the actor's. Because all emotions involve physical expression, this sensorimotor coupling between actor and spectator helps the spectator to read the mind of the performer in a matter of milliseconds. In the next phase of empathy, called 'imaginary transposition' by Thompson, the spectator puts him or herself into the shoes of the actor to begin to understand why the actor is registering this emotion. In this case, the spectator will likely form some tentative hypotheses about the actor/character's intentions on the basis of his or her anger within the dramatic situation. (Of course, the actor could also be angry because her partner on stage dropped a line or the board operator missed a light cue, but these are less likely suppositions.) Sensorimotor coupling works together with imaginary transposition to facilitate the early stages of empathy – to allow one person to sense the emotions and read the intentions of another. There are other levels of empathy, but these first two are the levels most frequently encountered in the theatre. As Thompson relates, we engage in these cognitive operations hundreds of times each day, as we try to read the minds of others to negotiate our social world.

For our evolving species, empathy and the sociality it fostered had obvious survival benefits. Sensorimotor coupling helped hominids to intuit others' movements and emotions; the cognitive process provided a kind of social attunement necessary for many cooperative efforts, such as hunting and starting fires. Not surprisingly, many higher mammals that travel in herds or socialize in bands also seem to possess some rudimentary mirror neurons. Imaginary transposition, however, appears to be much more limited in other species. Human children begin to engage in this cognitive operation at about nine to twelve months of age, when they first sense that other people are intentional creatures like themselves. Knowing that others were 'like me' must have helped hominids to work toward better modes of communication and probably provided one of the cognitive bases for altruism. Unlike any other species, humans sometimes sacrifice themselves for non-relatives. Empathy, then, helped to make our ancestors the most social and potentially the most cooperative of the higher mammals.

Empathy also fostered emotional and affective communication. The primary human emotions, facilitated by the limbic part of the brain, include fear, panic, joy, rage, care, disgust, and curiosity. Each of these emotions is sparked by specific stimuli, which trigger a chemical response and the activation of dedicated neuronal networks in the brain. These changes lead, in turn, to changes in muscle tone, blood flow, and hormonal response. While most psychologists understand emotions as directed at someone or something ('I'm angry at Fred'), they usually define affects as non-directed moods and feelings ('I'm depressed today'). All affects and emotions are a matter of degree – some level of affect is a normal part of everyday life. Human beings don't simply 'get emotional'; our bodies are constantly experiencing emotions and affects. In addition, these emotions and affects always take time to run their course in our bodies and brains. Evolution primed us to produce emotions and affects automatically and unconsciously to enable survival. Panic would send a hominid child who wandered too far from the band back to her relatives. Disgust might warn a hominid man who sniffed last night's cooked meat not to eat it again. If survival were at stake for the whole band, a general mood of anxiety might be warranted. Or take joy. Perhaps three members of a hominid band started to decorate each other with the ends of burnt sticks, and then one beat on a log with an old bone and the other two began dancing. Others in the band came to watch, standing or sitting in places that afforded a good view, and the mutual joy the participants took in their actions kept the two dancing until sundown.

In addition to the primary emotions, actors and spectators often experience social emotions. Social emotions are generally tied to the imaginary transposition of empathy. If we are aware that others are making assumptions about our emotions and intentions as a result of their ability to take our perspective on a situation, we may easily become embarrassed by what we believe they are thinking. Embarrassment is one of several social emotions that typically spring from imaginary transposition. Other social emotions include admiration, guilt, envy, sympathy, indignation, and pride. According to many psychologists, the social emotions, unlike the primary ones, depend upon cultural conditioning as well as evolution and heredity for their development and expression. Other higher mammals also display some social emotions, but they are more important in our species. In the 'get thee to a nunnery' scene with Ophelia, when she seeks to return some 'remembrances' that he has given to her, Hamlet clearly suffers from embarrassment and pride. The actor playing the prince may also choose to color some of his lines in the scene with guilt, indignation, and/or sympathy. I will examine how actors work with emotions and how spectators experience them in more detail in the next two sections.

Conceptual integration

While empathy, affect, and emotion are important cognitive processes that help to constitute playing in the theatre, they are hardly sufficient. These cognitive capabilities shape the experiences of many higher animals, but other mammals cannot make theatre or perceive the activities of their cohorts as a performance. The significant difference between us and other animals with regard to performance is our ability to engage in a high level of conceptual integration. Conceptual integration, also called 'conceptual blending', facilitates many aspects of human cognition, from our ability to use grammar and language to our understanding of analogies and cause–effect processes. Other animals cannot do the kind of blending that humans manage with ease.

Regarding performance, the key contribution made by conceptual integration is role-playing. To describe this process
at its most fundamental level, when an actor plays a character, she is able to blend a concept of herself with a concept
of the character to be played.

How is this possible? To begin with, conceptual integration depends on our ability to think with concepts. 'By
concept', say neuroscientists Gerald Edelman and Guilio
Tononi, 'we mean the ability to combine different perceptual categorizations related to a scene or an object and to
construct a "universal" reflecting the abstraction of some
common feature across a variety of precepts' (*A Universe of
Consciousness*, 2000, p. 104). They give as an example the
human face, which we all recognize as the same concept,
regardless of the many different eyes, mouths, shades of
skin, and so on that we perceive in discrete, unique combinations; 'face' is the universal concept uniting these distinct
precepts. Similarly, 'self' is a universal concept learned in
infancy and shared by all humanity, although different cultures define the concept in different ways. Many concepts are
based on cognitive primitives that infants learn by exploring
the affordances of their environments. Through everyday,
bodily experience, infants learn the difference between up
and down and come to understand that some objects can
contain other objects. These perceptual affordances lead to
such basic concepts as 'standing' and 'cup' and may even
eventuate in metaphorical expressions such as 'an upright
man' and 'contain your anger', which are extensions of the
conceptual primitives 'up/down' and 'containment'. The

slate of our minds is not blank when we emerge as new-borns; our neurons are already partly organized to facilitate survival, and this organization includes the seeds of foundational concepts for later enculturation.

With regard to role-playing, the cognitive foundation of theatre and performance, children begin playing games of make-believe sometime after they are two years old. The basic concepts involved in such play are 'self' and 'role', which the child will have internalized about a year before when he began to distinguish between 'me' and 'others like me' to enable the imaginary transposition of empathy. During the intervening year or so, the child will have built up a much better memory of the daily activities of significant others in his life by mimicking those actions in play and remembering their salient features. In a famous series of experiments, psychologist John Gerstmyer videotaped the make-believe play activities of his toddler daughter and her playmates over several months. Gerstmyer's tapes reveal that his daughter and her friends engaged in all of the major activities that we associate with the staging of drama while they 'played house' together. His daughter acted the role of her mother, for example, by adopting a slow and emphatic speech pattern. In what we might call a move toward dramatic economy, the children even foreshortened the usual time it would take to perform many dramatic actions. When toddler/mother cooked a meal on a pretend stove, she shook the pot and said 'cook cook' to speed up cooking time, for instance. Gerstmyer's daughter frequently stepped out of her role to become an announcer or a stage manager of her actions, temporarily treating her playmates as spectators. She and her friends also created 'special effects' for their improvisations, vocalizing a 'vroom vroom' sound while 'driving' in the car. Occasionally the toddlers dropped their back-stage and on-stage roles to become audience members, enjoying a giggle together about what they had created before moving back into their fiction.

Although we tend to take such interactions among two-year-olds for granted, what Gerstmyer's toddler and her friends created is really quite extraordinary. No other animal can do this. The development of young chimps is quite similar to that of humans until both are about a year and a half old. Then humans begin to master language and other forms of conceptual complexity, including role-playing, and whole worlds open up to us that are forever closed to other animals. It took millions of years of evolution to enable Gerstmyer's toddler to embody the role of her mother within a play frame that she could manipulate as a make-believe event.

Specifically, the kind of world available to human children when they play 'let's pretend' is a subjunctive one. In English grammar, 'subjunctive' designates a verb form expressing contingent or hypothetical action. Whenever people build a model to explore how something might work, play a computer game that involves the participant in virtual reality, or perform a dramatic fiction for others, they engage in subjunctive action. In *An Actor Prepares* (1936), Konstantin Stanislavski invites actors to participate in a conditional, virtual world when he invokes what he calls 'the magic if'.

The question 'If I were this character in that situation, what would I do?' – one understanding of Stanislavski's 'magic if' – is the basis for the actor's imaginative investment in the subjunctive world of the play. It is also, of course, the essence of the implicit contract between actors and spectators that makes theatre possible. 'Let's pretend that a prince returns to Denmark to find his father dead and his uncle on the throne' is the conditional 'if' that allows actors and spectators to play together to create *Hamlet*. Gerstmyer's toddler would have understood.

In their book *The Way We Think* (2002), Gilles Fauconnier and Mark Turner note the experiments behind conceptual blending, explain how it works, and discuss several instances of it in operation, including the theatre. When actors create roles, they take parts of their own concept of themselves and combine it with their concept of the role they are performing. An actor performing Blanche DuBois in *A Streetcar Named Desire* will combine certain elements of herself – a possible voice, walk, and mode of gesturing, for example – with the words and actions that Tennessee Williams has given to her character. Spectators also engage in conceptual integration. While watching the actor play Blanche in *Streetcar*, they will take selected content from the actor – that she can move and speak in specific ways, for instance – and combine it with their concept of the character – that Blanche has a certain past and faces specific conflicts in the present. Notice that blending is always selective; all conceptual integrations take only parts of their initial concepts, according to Fauconnier and Turner. The actor will certainly know that Blanche goes crazy at the end of the play, but must not allow her awareness of this fact to intrude on her moment-to-moment playing of the character. The spectator could think about the actor's life outside of this stage role, but usually puts such knowledge aside to focus on the actor as character. For most of the action of the play, actors and spectators will live in their blends to enjoy the flow of the performance.

But not for all of it. Like Gerstmyer's toddler, actors and spectators can choose to stay within the dramatic frame of the play or they can temporarily un-blend their actor/character integrations and leave the fiction behind. If a spectator hears someone snoring beside her, she can pull back from her involvement in the blends of the play to nudge the offender awake. Similarly, the actor might temporarily drop his self/character blend to hold for a laugh. Occasionally, mistakes — forgetting a line or dropping a prop — will momentarily propel both actors and spectators out of their blends. Actors and spectators with a lot of theatrical experience will usually oscillate in and out of their blends throughout a performance. Actors will find moments when they can quickly shift their attention from the immediate circumstances of their character to tune into the response of the audience. And spectators who have watched a performer several times before will sometimes drop the imagined actor/character blend to focus solely on the performer's vocal or physical skill. Just as Gerstmyer's toddler could switch from role-playing to stage managing to spectating in the midst of her improvising, grown-up acting and spectating in the theatre invite such oscillation among discrete roles and blends. The activities of the theatre encourage its participants to think about the inherent doubleness of all theatricality.

The creation of a theatrical character may involve more than one performer engaging in conceptual blending. In kathakali dance-drama, begun in seventeenth-century India and still practiced today, dramatic characters emerge through the cooperation of an actor-dancer, the vocalist who is singing his dialogue, and the percussionists who accompany the action. During a kathakali production, the audience blends inputs from all of these performers to create the character and to interpret his (all performers are male) actions. While the body of the actor-dancer remains the foundation for all kathakali characters in performance, audiences need not see a complete human body to imagine a dramatic character. In traditional Japanese bunraku puppetry, spectators use conceptual integration to blend inputs from a puppet, typically three to four feet tall, and three adult male manipulators, who move the doll's head, arms, and feet.

Peter Schumann, artistic director of The Bread and Puppet Theater in the United States, has taken the bunraku notion of puppet manipulation to new heights. Some of the puppets he and his associates stage in his parades stand over twenty feet high and require five manipulators for their arms, legs, and bodies. Audiences have enjoyed watching the coordination of the animators as well as seeing the long arms of puppets such as Uncle Fatso (a capitalist-exploiter dressed like Uncle Sam) reach out over the audience as the puppets march along. With bunraku and Schumann's

Warthose?

of ?

puppets, the agency for the creation of a character is shared among several animators, but the operation of conceptual integration is the same for the audience as it is with the creation of one character by a single actor. In both cases, spectators rely on the basic cognitive operation of role-playing that integrates inputs from different concepts – the 'self' or 'selves' of one or several actors who can move, speak, and so on, plus the concept of a 'role' in a script or scenario that seeks certain intentions within a given situation – to create a selves/role blend.

Fauconnier and Turner, who elaborate the ramifications of conceptual blending in many areas of human activity, estimate that *Homo sapiens* began to fully practice this cognitive operation about fifty thousand years ago. Around that time, human culture exploded as modern humans migrated out of Africa and into Asia and Europe. Anthropologists have found evidence of sophisticated tools, cave drawings, and musical instruments from that era. Some scientists believe that language and religious rituals also began at that time. It is evident that when conceptual integration gave our ancestors the cognitive flexibility to play roles in subjunctive events, it allowed us to extend what had earlier been hominid playing into fully human performing. Roughly fifty thousand years ago, culture became the primary locus for human innovation and we no longer had to wait for the slow process of genetic evolution to provide more possibilities. Or, as Fauconnier and Turner put it, 'The great evolutionary change that produced cognitively modern human beings was a matter of evolving an organism that could run off-line cognitive simulations so that evolution did not have to undertake the tedious process of natural selection every time a choice was to be made' (*The Way We Think*, p. 217). Conceptual integration and the ability to build subjunctive worlds did not free us from biology – blending still requires living, embodied minds – but it did allow our species to elaborate human cultures upon a common biological foundation.

Performativity

At this point in our discussion, some critics might complain that when we blend concepts to create possible worlds, the end result is still hypothetical. The blends in a performance (or in an architectural drawing or a scientific experiment) can help us to think about models and to consider alternatives for the future, but – such critics might say – virtual reality is not truly real. This was the position of the philosopher J. L. Austin, who focused on what he took to be the differences between speech acts that made something happen in the real world and others that did not. Austin coined the term 'performative' in 1955 to apply narrowly to a particular kind of utterance in everyday speech that causes a change in the material world. When a minister says to a couple in a church, 'I now pronounce you husband and wife', for example, she has uttered a performative statement. Noting that an actor playing a minister on stage could not actually marry anyone, Austin distinguished performative language from language used in a theatrical fiction. Austin's discussion of performativity has led some later thinkers to rule out action on the stage, as well in film, on television, and in related media, as a possible cause of change in the world. In contrast, other theorists argue that fictional actions can be just as real as actions in everyday life.

From an evolutionary and cognitive perspective, Austin's distinction between performative utterances and fictitious statements that have no real-world results was misleading. All modes of speech are actions, and all actions, even those that are part of a subjunctive world, have consequences. When actors and spectators use mental concepts and integrate some of them into blends, they alter their own and others' neuronal connections. Our brains are a part of the real world; experiences, even fictitious ones, mess with the materiality of our minds. To think otherwise is to back into the Cartesian fallacy, which posits a separation between our minds and our bodies. In this sense, all theatre is performative; it certainly makes things happen in the real world of our minds and may help to cause other material changes as well. The consequences of conceptual blending in the theatre may not be earth-shaking, but few real experiences are. Nonetheless, subjunctive thinking can lead to innovation because blending allows people to borrow parts of concepts and put them together in new combinations. African American actors, for example, can play Caucasian characters, and the casting of whole plays can mix genders, races, and sexual orientations in challenging ways. And casting, of course, is only one of many strategies that theatre artists can use to play around with conventional stereotypes and ideas.

Our evolutionary heritage, recapitulated in the childhood development of all *Homo sapiens*, has endowed us with the ability to participate in a wide range of performances, including the theatre. This participation necessarily involves embodiment and embeddedness, in our minds, in our bodies, and in the affordances of our environments. Like their hominid ancestors, actors in the theatre create specific patterns of action (primarily through speech and movement) that induce spectators to pay attention to them. Empathy, affect, and emotion are fundamental to these games of pattern and attention. Similar to other higher mammals, participants in the theatre set their play events apart from their other daily activities. Although animal play continues to be an important foundation of all theatre, *Homo sapiens* broke from their evolutionary cousins about fifty thousand years ago when they acquired the ability to do double-scope conceptual integration. Only when blending allowed humans to perform temporary roles in invented, subjunctive situations could our ancestors transform general playing into human performing. This shift facilitated the proliferation of many kinds of performing, including the theatre.

Acting

Mind and body

Current practitioners and theorists of acting can be divided into two broad camps – those who emphasize the mental and psychological aspects of the art and those who explore the physical and kinesthetic side of acting. Within this general dichotomy there are two extremes – theorists who continue to worship at the shrine of Method Acting and others who preach the necessity of Physical Theatre. Most near the psychological end of the continuum believe that the proper 'internal' psychological exercises will draw the body along with the mind, while those near the other end believe that 'external' physical work can bend the mind to the body. It would be nice to be able to say that the truth lies somewhere in between. But in fact both positions are misconceived; both depend upon a dualism that does not exist.

Nonetheless, this dualism is difficult to escape or even consciously resist. As philosopher Mark Johnson notes, 'Mind/body dualism is so deeply embedded in our philosophical and religious traditions, in our shared conceptual systems, and in our language that it can seem to be an inescapable fact about human nature' (*The Meaning of the Body*, 2007, p. 2). He points out that the mind/body dichotomy carries over into many other ways of dividing our experience of the world – 'cognition/emotion, fact/value, knowledge/ imagination, and thought/feeling' (p. 7). In the previous section, however, we have already seen that the mind and the body are intertwined and inseparable in the operations of empathy, emotion, and conceptual blending; all three involve an embodied mind and a body that could be called 'mind-full'. In fact, philosopher Maxine Sheets-Johnstone uses this term, 'the mind-full body', to denote the complete integration of human bodies and minds as they experience their lives (quoted in John Lutterbie's *Toward a General Theory of Acting*, 2011, p. 24). As we will see, recognizing this integration is also a good foundation for understanding actors as they perform on the stage.

Stanislavski knew that actors needed to bridge the mind/body divide and coined the term 'psycho-physical' to describe his approach to performance training. Other western acting teachers and theorists, including Michael Chekhov and Jacques Lecoq, have also understood the need for actors to integrate mind-full bodies with body-full minds. Such is the pull of the mind/body dualism on our language and on our ways of writing about acting, however, that even these practitioner-theorists have not always found locutions that avoid the dichotomy. Nonetheless, this section will draw on some of their ideas, along with relevant insights from several cognitive scientists, to discuss actor training, improvising, and rehearsing. These three practices are not entirely discrete, of course; embodied techniques and strategies learned in each of them will usefully inform the practice of the other two. The gradual creative growth that actors experience by moving from training to improvising to rehearsing, however, does trace the general path of many performers, and each of these steps has distinctive goals. Consequently, we can discuss each practice in this three-part process somewhat separately.

Actor training

Regarding training, we should begin by acknowledging that actors have inherited mind–body capabilities for movement from our ancestors on the evolutionary tree that are mostly self-regulating. Like other higher animals, actors have an innate sense of the positioning of their own bodies. They do not have to be observing their arms, for example, to know whether they are crossed or at their sides. Physiologists call this 'proprioception', and we are born with this capability. Soon after birth, infants use their vision and hearing to extend proprioceptive awareness by exploring their surroundings. Through early proprioception and interaction, individuals build up a concept of their bodies that cognitive philosopher Shaun Gallagher calls a 'body schema'. State Gallagher and his co-author Dan Zahavi, '[T]he body schema is a system of sensorimotor capacities and activations that function without the necessity of perceptual monitoring. ... [T]he normal adult, in order to move around and act in the world, neither needs nor has a constant body percept that takes the body as an object' (*The Phenomenological Mind*, 2008, p. 146). That is, we do not need to think about our muscles, tendons, blood flow, nerves, and so on to be able to engage them in most actions; the body schema is nearly always unconscious. Through proprioception and body schema, brain and body unite to give most of us a foundational sense of our identity and an ability to move with purpose and efficiency. These embodied processes allow us to walk across the street without pausing to consider how we will put one foot in front of the other.

Nonetheless, as Stanislavski recognized, beginning actors often have trouble walking across the stage. This is because the body schema, though generally unconscious in operation, is linked to intentional action. Actors who do not know their intentions – why their characters are walking across the stage, for example – will tend to falter in their movements. Gallagher identifies four ways of moving: reflex, locomotive, instrumental, and expressive. Only reflex movement involves no intention and no activation of our body schemas. Locomotive movement (getting from here to there by walking, climbing, crawling, etc.) and instrumental movement (performing a task by writing, grasping, pushing, driving, etc.) rely on body schema and proprioception. As long as actors know the reason behind the action, their mind-full bodies can usually get from here to there and perform simple tasks on stage without their thinking about how these acts are to be accomplished. Take away the intention, the goal for the action, however, and the body schema cannot do its work unconsciously. The usual result for actors is self-consciousness and awkwardness. The lesson here for movement training is that it must be linked to playing intentions; actors need strong, flexible bodies, but simply working out in the gym is not enough. Stanislavski understood this body–mind connection and most beginning acting classes based on his teachings help students to generate movements for their characters through the embodiment of intentions.

Gallagher calls his fourth mode of movement 'expressive'. Unlike simple locomotion or the performance of tasks, expressive movement is intended to communicate to others. Although interpersonal communication can inflect locomotive and instrumental movements, expressive movement has its own dynamics and is usually infused with emotion. One cognitive foundation for this type of movement is what

Gallagher calls a person's 'body image'. This is more conscious than a body schema and, consequently for the actor, more controllable. Notes Gallagher, 'The body image, consisting of a complex set of mental representations, involves a form of explicit and self-referential intentionality' (p. 216). At its simplest, your body image is how you feel about yourself when looking in a mirror. This means your body image changes depending on multiple internal and external stimuli – illness, exercise, concerns about weight and appearance, and so on. How we feel about our bodies may depend more on the values and ideologies advanced by the major institutions of our culture – religion, sports, the food industries, pharmaceutical companies, and similar institutions and their messages in the United States, for instance – than on what our bodies are telling us through internal signals. Overall, body image combines our perceptual experience of our own body, our emotional attitude toward it, and our conceptual understanding of bodies in general. Our expressive movements typically reflect and embody our present body image. Others can tell if you think of yourself as shy, sexy, distracted, threatened, confident, or belligerent, say, on the basis of your posture and movement.

Because actors know that much of what they communicate about their characters depends upon how they move, they seek some conscious control over the body image they project on stage. An actor performing Blanche DuBois in *Streetcar* will want to alter her body image to be able to express the bossy, hopeful, broken, and sexual sides of Blanche. As this example suggests, some complex characters have several potential body images, while others, such as the stock figures in commedia dell'arte, can best be played by emphasizing a single dominant mode of embodiment. Lecoq's regimen of physical training seeks to extend the range of expressivity that actors can embody through their movement. To focus their attention on physical expressiveness, Lecoq requires his actors to perform many of his initial exercises without speaking. Regarding his general goals, Lecoq states, 'The dynamics underlying my teaching are those of the relationship between rhythm, space, and force. The laws of movement have to be understood on the basis of the human body in motion: balance, disequilibrium, opposition, alternation, compensation, action, reaction. These laws may all be discovered in the body of a spectator as well as of the actor' (*The Moving Body*, 2001, p. 21). For example, Lecoq involves his actors in a series of exercises that work with the 'opposition' of 'push' and 'pull'. Actors explore in action what it means to push and be pushed, to pull and be pulled. And later, after they have grounded this work in their bodies, actors explore the differences between pushing with words while the body is pulled back. This could relate to a dramatic situation in which a character pushed out words to say she was unafraid at the same time that her body delivered a very different message. The actor playing Blanche in the rape scene at the end of *Streetcar*, for instance, may choose to emphasize this opposition between body and voice as that scene nears its climax.

For Lecoq, the opposition between push and pull is one of 'the laws of movement' and it is applicable to all human beings. Significantly, cognitive scientists dealing with language, emotions, and meaning validate Lecoq's intuition about the strong link between intentional physicality and emotional communication. Mark Johnson, drawing on the scholarship of Sheets-Johnstone, broadens our usual understanding of 'meaning' to embrace insights about embodiment that Lecoq understood through his work with actors. States Johnson, 'The key to my entire argument is that meaning is not just what is consciously entertained in acts of feeling and thought; instead, meaning reaches deep down into our corporeal encounter with our environment. ... At some point, these meanings-in-the-making ("proto-meanings" or "immanent meanings," if you will) can be consciously appropriated, and it is only then that we typically think of something as "meaningful to us"' (*The Meaning of the Body*, p. 25). Such meanings for actors, working on their own bodies and interacting with others within a stage environment, are prompted by their sensorimotor engagements. To describe these different kinds of engagement, Johnson uses terms that are very close to those of Lecoq: 'tension', 'linearity', 'amplitude', and 'projection'.

In addition to training their voices for breath support, articulation, and resonance, actors must explore and extend the gestural side of speech. Gestures are any movements made by the upper body (which can include the head and face as well as the shoulders, arms, and hands) that are linked to an utterance. Recent research into vocal utterance confirms the co-expressive nature of speech and gesture. According to neuroscientist David McNeill, 'Utterances possess two sides, only one of which is speech; the other is imagery, actional and visuo-spatial. To exclude the gesture side, as has been traditional, is tantamount to ignoring half of the message out of the brain' (*Language and Gesture*, 2000, p. 69). From an evolutionary point of view, hominid gestures preceded spoken language; consequently, it should not be surprising that the images-in-action created by gestures continue to complement speech. To explore this for yourself, look in a mirror and use speech to describe something round or someone moving quickly and watch what your arms and hands do naturally, as you are talking.

When actors say that they do not know what to do with their hands, it is usually because they have not fully embodied the language of the role they are playing; they have not made the transition from a printed script to the spoken utterance of a character in action. Critics sometimes describe beginning actors as 'wooden' on stage because they are all talk and no gesture. Many of Lecoq's exercises can help actors to integrate these complementary sides of communicating. Lecoq understood that actors must find those points in their actions when they have a new idea and the urgency to communicate it erupts in the flowering of both speech and gesture. Similarly, long before performance teachers knew any cognitive science, Chekhov advised actors: 'Train yourself to make certain gestures with the utmost expressiveness, as fully and completely as you can. These gestures might express, for instance, drawing, pulling, pressing, lifting, throwing, crumpling, coaxing, separating, tearing, penetrating, touching, brushing away, opening, closing, breaking, taking, giving, supporting, holding back, scratching' (*To the Actor*, 1985, p. 41). Actors can make these gestures silently or, better yet, work them into an improvisation in which they are using speech as well as gestures to interact with a partner.

Improvisation

As Chekhov's advice implies, there is no clear break between training and improvisation. Nor, in many situations, between improv work and rehearsing. An improvisation is an open-ended exercise that specifies the circumstances of a dramatic situation involving two or more actor/characters but does not prescribe the outcome of the conflict between them. Acting teachers use improvs to encourage students to stretch their dramatic imaginations, and directors deploy them with their cast members to sharpen intentions and explore characterizations. Sometimes whole companies use improvisations to create a devised piece of theatre together.

At a minimum, improvs require conceptual integration and empathy. Actors must blend parts of themselves with aspects of their fictional roles and adopt the point of view of their characters. In addition, they must take, as a given, the characterizations adopted by their fellow actors and interact with them on the basis of how well their own character is able to read their fellow actors' emotions and intentions in the improvised situation. Even if they are playing characters very close to themselves in movement, speech, and general psychology, they will find that the given situation and their

intentions within it already place them in an 'as if', subjunctive condition, and playing it out demands that they remain
consistent in terms of the 'who', 'what', 'where', and 'when'
of their situation.

In improvisations where the goal is to build sensitivities
and capacities that will culminate in the performance of a
specific role in a scene or a full play, actors may use some
of Chekhov's exercises to help them with problems of conceptual integration and empathy. In *The Path of the Actor*,
Chekhov notes, 'If an actor prepares his role correctly, the
whole process of preparation can be characterized by his
gradual approach to the picture of his character as he sees it
in his imagination, in his fantasy. The actor first builds up his
character exclusively in his fantasy life, then tries to imitate
the character's inner and outer qualities' (2005, p. 108).
Chekhov's imagined character, of course, is the same as the
concept of a role that Fauconnier and Turner describe when
they discuss how the actor blends self and role together in
the process of conceptual integration. Imitating that character's imagined qualities, as Chekhov recommends, will lead
the actor to embody an actor/character blend, the conceptual basis of performance for Fauconnier and Turner . Like
Johnson, Chekhov understood that such imitation might
begin in the imagination but had to be grounded in the
body. If the actor attempts to physically imitate an imagined
moving figure, she will spark low-level empathy, because
the mirror neurons of the actor will mentally mirror the
movements of the figure. Working from imagination to
physicalization through trial and error over time will also

allow the actor to build one or several body images that are appropriate for the character. In this way, through improvising and rehearsing, the actor gradually transforms herself into a fully embodied actor/character.

As the actor uses empathy to move toward a blended characterization, perception, attention, and executive control become more important. As previously noted, perception is not a matter of taking in the world through the senses and then sorting through this mountain of impressions until you get the information you need. If it were, our species would have died off eons ago: Action for survival often depends on immediate response. Instead, perception is a pro-active search engine that focuses on only a small fraction of our surroundings – those parts of it that have relevance to our immediate well-being and intentions. Even with perception ignoring most of reality, much of what we perceive in everyday life registers at the unconscious level and does not require our attention. This is true also in improvisation, but creating an 'as if' situation through blending and empathy invariably requires a heightening of the activity of attention. According to many of the cognitive scientists who have studied it, attention is a lot like a follow-spot with an adjustable opening, allowing us to take in more or less of a visual field. Attention also works for sound, and in this regard it is a little like a directional microphone that picks up only the sounds at which it is aimed. Attention involves consciousness, and this requires the more highly evolved areas of our brains, which include working memory, to move into high gear. By engaging consciousness, the brain is able to put together fleeting representations of our immediate circumstances.

Of course, it is not enough simply to attend to the evolving circumstances of an improvisation. Improvs also demand that actors make some decisions and take action on the basis of these unstable neural representations. This calls into play what many neuroscientists call the 'executive function' of our brains. Located in the neo-cortex, executive control is networked to many other areas of the brain, including the sensory–motor and emotional processing areas; it both sends and receives neural activations. Through complex processes that neuroscientists are only beginning to understand, the executive brain synthesizes cues from the environment, from relevant memories, and from other networked activations to make split-second decisions about possible courses of action. This involves scanning memory for a possible fit between a past solution and present circumstances. Usually an earlier precedent will help to resolve a present problem, but novel solutions occasionally emerge when a new neural network is slotted into an existing pattern. In his *Toward a General Theory of Acting*, John Lutterbie summarizes this process: 'Through exercising executive control, [the actor] attends to certain types of information and recalls experiences that bear a resemblance to current circumstances. As obstacles are encountered alternative behaviors are tested until one is found that solves the problem or a compromise is reached. ... [T]hrough attention and executive control emerging patterns are tested, embraced or rejected, until a sequence of actions is deemed acceptable' (p. 111). All of this must occur on the fly, in a matter of milliseconds, during the heat of an improvisation. As we will see, the same process occurs hundreds of times over several rehearsals as actors work to build up a performance score.

As noted in the previous section, empathizing with others nearly always calls forth emotions. At the same time as actors are working toward fully embodied characterizations, they are also attempting to read the emotions of the other actor/characters with whom they are improvising. Improvisations, whether in a class or in rehearsals for a production, provide a unique opportunity to explore emotion. We have already seen that intended movements and gestures can arouse emotions; in fact, they are generally more important than specific words in activating emotional response. If a good actor repeats the phrase 'I love you' and links it to movements and gestures that embody hatred, disgust, fear, and other negative emotions, the actor will begin to experience those negative emotions, not the care and desire usually expressed by the words alone.

One of the strongest ways for humans to 'gesture' is through the facial muscles. Psychologist Paul Ekman has been working on the relations among facial expressions and emotions for decades. As Ekman relates, 'I found that when I made certain expressions, I was flooded with strong emotional sensations. It wasn't just any expression, only the ones I had already identified as universal to human beings' (*Emotions Revealed*, 2003, p. 37). Since then, Ekman and his researchers have developed charts that link specific facial expressions to specific primary emotions. People from cultures around the world will usually identify the same faces as happy, angry, or sad, even though each culture constrains the acceptable public expression of our primary emotions. Ekman also discovered that the activation of vocal muscles to create emotional sounds produced those internal emotions in the person doing the vocalizing. Note that emotions generated through both face and voice have to do with controllable musculature. This means that actors can consciously manipulate their muscles to produce real emotions.

In contrast, many US actors, especially those trained in Method techniques, believe that the only way to activate genuine emotion is through memory. Empirical studies do indicate that a strong emotional memory linked to an episode in the actor's past can help to generate that emotion in the present, but such memories seem to work on emotions by activating a muscular response in the body of the actor. Regardless of the acting technique, the crucial link is between embodiment and emotion, with memory serving primarily as a stimulus to the sensorimotor–emotion system. The point is that actors have at least two ways to generate emotions in themselves, and both involve their muscles. When Anna Deavere Smith was rehearsing in New York City for her one-woman production *Fires in the Mirror* (1992), a play about conflict and rioting between Hasidic Jews and Afro-Caribbean Americans, she created the emotions of her characters directly through the conscious activation of her vocal, postural, and gestural muscles. Smith had interviewed all of the people she would later portray in her solo performance, and her primary rehearsal technique was to precisely imitate the voices of those she had recorded. Later, when she tried to teach this technique to students, many objected that getting to know these people from the inside was better than simple external imitation. But Smith objected: 'My argument was, and still is, that it does not have to be either/or, and that neither comes first. The discovery of human behavior can happen in motion. It can be a process of moving from the self to the other and the other to the self. ... I knew that by using another person's language, it was possible to portray what was invisible about that person' (p. xxxii). As actor and theatre scholar Richard Kemp affirms, Smith's repeated vocalization of speech patterns in rehearsal 'calls to mind Paul Ekman's observation that the consciously chosen use of an emotion can generate the experience of that emotion' ('Embodied Acting', 2010, p. 140). Actually, working up emotions through imitation or through memory is not really an either/or proposition in terms of our mindful bodies. Both techniques involve animating an emotional response through the sensorimotor system; one method is simply more direct than the other.

Rehearsal

Memory is central, however, when actors use the rehearsal process to gradually put together a performance score. As the term implies, actors break up their performances into specific units of action and 'score' each of them, much as a composer and conductor decide on the shape, pace, and tone of a unit of music. Although most scripts provide the rough outline of a general score for the actor, she or he still has many decisions to make, especially with regard to interacting with other actor/characters within the environment on stage. Psychologists have defined several kinds of memory, and many of these come into play as actors work through scoring possibilities during rehearsals. In terms of two broad categories of memory, actors aim to offload as much of their performance as they can from explicit onto implicit memory. Explicit memory takes conscious attention; actors who must think 'What's my next line?' and 'Where do I sit down after I say this?' are struggling with explicit memory. In contrast, professional actors master techniques over the years that help them to rely on implicit, unconscious memory; they learn their lines quickly, link them with the on-stage movement of their character, and intertwine both with intentions and responses.

Moving stage action from explicit to implicit memory is especially important for safe and effective fight scenes. In a production of *Hamlet*, the actors playing Hamlet and Laertes will probably begin work on the dueling scene that ends the tragedy very early in rehearsals. With a fight coach, they will build every move of their sword play together, try out alternative possibilities, set it early on, and likely go over it a hundred times before opening night. The more comfortable the performers become with their dueling – the more each can offload it from his explicit onto his implicit memory – the safer for both actors. Further, as the actors gain confidence they can allow more emotional engagement

to color their dueling, with the consequence that the fight
will probably seem more dangerous to the audience.

In order to build a sword fight or, indeed, to build any
dramatic scene together, actors must initially rely on short-
term or working memory. Short-term memory allows the
actor to retain a few key perceptions and normally lasts
from fifteen to thirty seconds. Think of what happens when
someone gives you a new telephone number: You can usually retain the number long enough to write it down or put
it into your cell phone, but after half a minute or so it has
vanished from your memory. The executive brain facilitates
short-term memory by attending to perceptual and/or proprioceptive information and then networking neurons so
that patterns emerge that allow for immediate retention and
repetition. But working memory is fleeting. When learning
some blocking or a new bit of business in rehearsal, actors
usually like to make a note of it in their scripts as well as
repeating it a few times so that the action can be recalled
later. After rehearsal, they may repeat the action again, in
their imagination, as they re-read their scripts to recall the
blocking. These techniques begin the process of consolidat-
ing intentional actions and gradually shift them from short-
term into long-term memory.

Long-term memory works in many parts of the brain
and usually depends on repetition, both embodied and
imagined, to be effective. Although people often think of
long-term memories as 'stored' images or sounds, we do
not have metaphorical file cabinets or hard drives in our
heads that allow us to pull out exactly what was put in some

time ago. Because neural networks are constantly re-wiring themselves in response to experience, there can be no 'storage area' unchanged by neural activity. For neuroscientist Gerald Edelman, 'constructive recategorization' is a better metaphor for long-term memory than storage. According to Edelman and his co-author Giulio Tononi, 'In a complex brain, memory [recall] results from a selective matching that occurs between ongoing, distributed neural activity and various signals coming from the world, the body, and the brain itself. The synaptic alterations that ensue affect the future responses of the individual brain to similar or different signals' (*A Universe of Consciousness*, p. 95). We are able to remember a person's name, for example, because of previous actions that prompted the brain, so that a similar signal at a later time engages a similar response. Because the brain is dynamic, memory works to recategorize close similarities, not to match up an exact perception with a stored one. All performances of long-term memory, even the recollection and speaking of a single word, engage different networks and firings each time.

Building a performance score requires actors to combine clear intentions with the minutiae of thousands of details in every area of performance – movement, speech, gesture, shifts in emotion, the manipulation of props, physical work with other actors, and perhaps some technical stage know-how (such as the aerial stunts in the 2011 New York production of *Spider-Man: Turn Off the Dark*). To do this efficiently, actors need to 'chunk' related bits of information together in their memory. That is, they need to put together strings of actions that occur over a short period of time and can be memorized as a coherent whole. A two-minute chunk of stage action, for example, might include five different strategies to win an argument with an opposing actor/character, with two or three blocking moves and the manipulation of a couple of props. Most chunks depend on a 'trigger'. Your character makes an entrance with important information, for example, and this triggers a sequence of actions. A memorable chunk usually has some psychological coherence and a clear arc of action, with a beginning and end. Actors chunk units of stage action, carefully craft and repeat each chunk in rehearsals, and gradually consolidate them in long-term memory. By the time of the last run-through before technical rehearsals, all the actor needs are the right circumstances and the 'trigger' to pursue and enact an entire chunk of stage action.

Actors need to score their performance and break it into memorable chunks regardless of the style of the play or production they are doing. Here is a passage from the opening of Heiner Müller's *Hamletmachine*, a 1977 postmodern play that invites the actor performing Hamlet to hold Shakespeare's character at a distance. After a mocking description of the beginning of his father's funeral, the actor playing Hamlet states:

> I stopped the funeral procession. I pried open the coffin with my sword, the blade broke, yet with the blunt remainder I succeeded and I dispensed my dead procreator FLESH LIKES TO

KEEP THE COMPANY OF FLESH among the bums around me. The mourning turned into rejoicing, the rejoicing into lip smacking, on top of the empty coffin the murderer humped the widow LET ME HELP YOU UP, UNCLE, OPEN YOUR LEGS, MAMA. I laid down on the ground and listened to the world doing its turns in step with the putrefaction. (1984, p. 53)

At the start of Müller's play, the performance of Shakespeare's tragedy is over. The actor, who tells the audience that he 'was Hamlet', already knows who killed his father, and he recalls an incident at the state funeral (above) that could not have occurred in the original play. At the same time, the actor gives voice to lines that parody some of Hamlet's speeches. (In Shakespeare's play after Hamlet kills Polonius, for example, the prince explains to Claudius how maggots and worms consume all corpses, with the consequence that a dead king 'may go a progress through the guts of a beggar'. Müller shortens this circuit by having his Hamlet cut up his father with a broken sword and distribute his flesh directly to the 'bums' at the funeral.) In addition to studying Müller's script, the actor, in order to begin to score this part of the opening monologue, will need to know Shakespeare's original play, the playwright Müller's social-political situation in East Germany in the 1970s, probably something about Müller's identification with the character of Hamlet, and perhaps some details about previous famous productions of *Hamlet*. Just to figure out what is going on in *Hamletmachine*, the actor will need help from the director and from a dramaturg who has done careful research. Nonetheless, in the end, the actor must make the same kinds of decisions as he would for a conventional, realist play about how to chunk his moment-to-moment actions in this passage in order to transform it into a memorable and playable sequence; the rehearsal task is the same.

Perhaps the trigger for this unit of dialogue and action is the actor's decision to share a joke with the audience about how he, as Hamlet, offended everybody at the funeral. Let's assume that the director and designer have given the actor a small platform onto which he can leap and that he jumps onto this platform, pretending it is his father's coffin, to stop the funeral procession. In pantomime, actor/Hamlet pries open the coffin and breaks his blade, but proceeds to carve up his 'father' anyway. He is still talking to the spectators about this until he comes to the words in capital letters in the script ('FLESH LIKES ... '), where the director and actor may decide that these were the actual words that Hamlet used at the funeral. When speaking these lines, then, the actor would shift in time and attitude from direct conversation with the audience in the theatre to an invitation to the bums, probably located on stage in his imagination. He stands up to address them in high oratorical style, but then returns to everyday speech with the spectators. Another quick shift, perhaps with a mocking laugh, and actor/Hamlet puts one foot down from the 'coffin' to offer a helping hand to his uncle ('LET ME HELP YOU ... '). Actor/Hamlet arranges the pantomimed bodies of Claudius and Gertrude on the coffin and finally stands over his imagined mother to spread her legs for his uncle. Then actor/Hamlet leaps off the coffin to gesture to the copulating bodies for the audience's benefit, as might a barker at a circus sideshow. Finally, in disgust, he stops laughing. His attempt at sharing a joke with the audience has failed; they (and he) are not amused. He walks downstage, and tells the spectators about the world's indifference (their own) to 'putrefaction' in Denmark. The chunk is over.

There are other possibilities for scoring this part of the opening monologue, of course, that might also provide the actor with a coherent narrative and a psychological path that makes its own grotesque sense. And that's the point. Chunks of action must make sense to the actor in order to be remembered, even though the actor (in this case) will know that the audience will be struggling for meaning during this opening scene.

Actors rely on several cognitive fundamentals to embody their performances. Like all participants in the subjunctive world of playing, they need conceptual integration and empathy, which necessarily involves their emotions. While actors can count on several unconscious processes for their work, such as proprioception and body schema, they must also train their body–mind for flexibility in crafting different body images and expressive gestures. Short-term and long-term memory are also foundational to the actor's art, allowing her to shape a performance score that relies primarily on recollected sequences of actions in implicit memory.

Spectating

Spectatorial multitasking

The notion that spectating in the theatre is somehow a matter of 'belief' remains an unfortunate cliché in most theatre criticism. In order for spectators to engage with actors as fictional characters in the theatre, repeat many critics, spectators must exercise their 'willing suspension of disbelief', the nineteenth-century dictum invoked by Samuel Taylor Coleridge. For Coleridge, watching actors embody characters was akin to a religious experience: Suspend 'disbelief' and what he called 'poetic faith' would flood in. A passionate theatregoer, Coleridge enjoyed performances of Hamlet and other Shakespearean heroes by the romantic actor Edmund Kean. Coleridge suggested that spectators had to consciously suspend their skepticism that Kean could actually be Hamlet so that the actor's genius could temporarily elevate them into an imagined realm where poetic faith could sustain Shakespeare's fiction.

Had Coleridge understood the cognitive dynamics of conceptual blending, he probably would have revised his thinking. Engaging with actors playing characters on the stage involves conceptual integration, not poetic faith. Spectators combine their mental concepts of a specific actor with a specific character to create blended actor/characters. Blending actors and characters is not an extraordinary ability involving a leap of faith; children playing house have the same capability and do it all the time, as we saw above. Coleridge emphasized the 'willing' suspension of skepticism, and spectators do need an initial spark of consciousness to begin playing the game of theatre. But once engaged in conceptual integration, spectators slip in and out of the blends of performance with little conscious thought. While watching *Hamlet*, spectators are implicitly invited to consider the skills of the actor playing the protagonist and the excellence of Shakespeare's poetic verse, in addition to blending both together to create a specific version of skillful actor/Shakespearean Hamlet. This means that spectators can move among at least three modes of attention while listening to the 'To be or not to be' soliloquy. They can admire Shakespeare's psychological shift in the phrase 'To sleep – perchance to dream', enjoy the actor's vocal and physical choices in playing that shift, or combine both into a blend to focus on actor/Hamlet's sudden realization that suicide is not an option. Such oscillation among modes of attention does involve milliseconds of human willing, but it has nothing to do with skepticism and faith.

Further, despite the importance of blending, other matters often intrude on the attention of spectators while they watch a performance. Spectators multitask while *Hamlet* (or any other performance) is moving forward. Within two minutes during the performance time of the Hamlet–Gertrude scene in Act III of the play, you as spectator might (1) enjoy actor/Hamlet demanding that his mother compare a picture of his father with her present husband, Claudius; (2) mentally step back from the immediate situation on stage to compare this particular actor's Hamlet with Kenneth Branagh's performance in the same scene; (3) take a moment to cross your legs; (4) admire the 's' sounds in Shakespeare's lines for Hamlet as he piles on his disgust with his mother's sexuality ('Nay, but to live / in the rank sweat of an enseamèd bed, / Stewed in corruption.'); (5) wonder at the shift in lighting that allowed the actor playing the Ghost to appear suddenly on stage without anyone seeing his entrance; (6) check your program to recall the names of the lighting and scene designers; (7) feel actor/Hamlet's growing anxiety as the actor/Ghost admonishes him to get on with his revenge; and (8) try to refocus your attention onto the stage after a spectator sitting behind you suddenly sneezes. Some of this spectator activity involves the blending and un-blending of actor/characters, but spectating is much more various than that. This description of two minutes of performance time already suggests that spectating involves conscious shifts in attention, empathy, emotions, narrative, theatrical conventions, memory, and cultural networks. Perhaps only half of the eight activities above will prove central to your enjoyment of the production, but any adequate understanding of spectating must be able to explain how and why all of them are possible.

Regarding empathy, it is clear from the previous discussion and the above examples that spectators normally empathize with several different people – some physically present, others imagined – during the course of a performance. The spectator above took the perspective of the actors on stage and perhaps an audience member (the sneezer) during those two minutes of performance time. In addition, our spectator also tried to figure out what some of the absent agents of the performance were up to: Why did Shakespeare craft some of his verse that way, and why did the director and designers make the choices they did? Theatregoing offers spectators the opportunity to put themselves in the shoes of many other people, past and present, in order to understand and judge their actions.

All of these figures have or had actual physical bodies. In contrast, spectators do not empathize directly with characters. By themselves, characters have no bodies; they are words on a page. A spectator who has read a play before coming to the theatre to watch it might imagine what a character looks and sounds like in his 'mind's eye' (and mind's ear) and empathize with that imagined body, but once inside the playhouse the former reader becomes an active spectator and the blend of a flesh-and-blood actor with the author's character always takes the place of the imagined figure in the reader's mind. Blending and empathizing are enjoyable for spectators. Empirical performance scholar Peter Eversmann and his students found that most theatregoers liked 'the feeling of being carried away by the performance, of losing oneself in the world of the stage, of forgetting everyday reality' ('The Experience of the Theatrical Event', 2004, p. 155). From a cognitive point of view, 'losing oneself' in the fiction of a play is impossible without blending and empathizing. Regardless of the kind of theatre they had just witnessed (farce, tragedy, musical comedy, etc.), spectators reported post-performance feelings to Eversmann that included 'admiration', 'joy', 'a true feast to go to', and 'very pleasurable to remember' (p. 155).

To understand these feelings, Eversmann deploys the idea of 'flow,' psychologist Mihaly Csikszentmihalyi's explanation for the pleasure humans take in playing and watching all kinds of performances. Borrowing from Csikszentmihalyi, Eversmann concludes that the spectators he and his students interviewed experienced 'a sense of concentration, of freedom, clarity, control, wholeness, and sometimes transcendence of ego boundaries' (p. 52). Understood in evolutionary terms, the experience of 'flow' is a general effect of playing; blending and empathizing at the playhouse allow spectators to experience joy when they 'go with the flow' of a performance. Evolution primed us for spectating and it rewards us with pleasurable feelings, not only in the theatre but at other performances, such as religious rituals and games of ice hockey. As we have seen, however, 'flow' does not occur throughout a performance. Audience attention in the theatre may be momentarily interrupted, or spectators may choose to stop the 'flow' of a performance by un-blending actor/characters to momentarily think about the work of such singular agents as actors, directors, and playwrights. But usually not for long. The pleasurable effects of 'flow' generally pull spectators back into the cognitive activities of blending and empathizing. Like Eversmann's interviewees, we enjoy immersing ourselves in the fictional world of the play, and blending and empathizing are the (mostly unconscious) cognitive operations that get us there.

Emotional engagement

While the pleasure deriving from 'flow' usually frames and informs our enjoyment of a complete performance event, spectators experience many other emotions in the course of watching a play. Theatre theorists and critics have been slow to adopt a method to understand spectator emotions, however, primarily because of a lingering commitment to semiotics in our discipline. Semiotics, the science of signs, directs scholars to narrow spectatorial activity to the reading of signs on stage. Despite clear psychological evidence that emotional engagement always informs the search for meaning, these scholars unscientifically assume that spectators are primarily engaged in trying to understand the symbolic meanings of a theatrical performance. Several investigators in film and television studies, however, begin with the assumption that emotional involvement is crucial for spectators when they experience and interpret a fictional film or television show. Among these scholars is Carl Plantinga, whose *Moving Viewers: American Film and the Spectator's Experience* (2009) builds on the insights of the cognitive sciences to understand how emotions inform the experience of film viewing. Not surprisingly, most of these insights are readily transferrable to understanding how our emotions guide us to make meaning during the performance of a drama in the theatre.

For a theatrical example, let's apply Plantinga's *Moving Viewers* to understand the likely emotional engagement of spectators enjoying Tony Kushner's two-part play *Angels in America* (1993, 1996). Kushner called his play 'A Gay

Fantasia on National Themes' and, indeed, it exposes and excoriates the anxieties, hypocrisies, and repressions of life in the United States during the Reagan era of the 1980s; the emotions it evokes are both harrowing and outrageously funny. Plantinga has good evidence that audience members experience some of their most intense and long-lasting emotions while watching major actor/characters adjust to significant shifts in a fiction's narrative. In addition to empathy, spectator curiosity and expectation pull us into the problems of actor/characters and we want to know what will happen next, says Plantinga. *Millennium Approaches*, the first part of *Angels*, quickly establishes the situation of two couples, Harper and Joe Pitt, a Mormon couple from Utah, recently married and now living in New York, and Prior Walter and Louis Ironson, a New York gay couple facing recent losses and worried about the AIDS epidemic. Both relationships are falling apart: Harper and Joe have problems in bed, and Louis freaks out when he discovers that Prior has AIDS. In two of the early turning points of the plot, Joe confesses that he is homosexual in a drunken, long-distance call to his mother in Utah, and Louis, terrified of catching AIDS from his boyfriend, abandons Prior. Although Kushner has carefully prepared the audience for both developments, most spectators will be surprised and saddened by these events. Plantinga terms this response to a turn in the narrative a 'direct' type of spectator emotion, and because the narrative of *Angels* takes many more twists and turns during its unfolding, spectators will experience many other direct emotions along the way.

More significant and longer-lasting than direct emotions are what Plantinga calls 'global' kinds of emotional responses. These are audience responses to major narrative developments that generally take several scenes to work through. Prior Walter's relationship with the Angel, for example – which begins with visitations by ghosts, involves an actual visitation from the Angel at the end of *Millennium Approaches*, and culminates in Prior's visit to Heaven in the second play, *Perestroika* – will likely evoke a global response in most spectators; its development takes the audience from curiosity to joy to sadness (with a mix of other emotions along the way). Hannah Pitt's (Joe's mother's) journey through both parts of the play also evokes global responses, as she finds the courage to change herself from an alienated Mormon housewife into a pro-active nurse for Prior and a mother figure for his friends. What happens to her shifts the audience from amusement to alarm, to relief, and eventually to joy. The final global experience of emotion occurs in the 'Epilogue' of *Perestroika*, when most of the saved but still wounded characters gather at the Bethesda fountain in Central Park in 1990, after the fall of the Berlin Wall. With the full weight of the play's several narratives embodied in these actor/characters' speeches and relationships, Kushner nonetheless achieves an emotional release for the audience that allows for a comic, guardedly optimistic ending. From Plantinga's perspective, direct emotional responses to single episodes can also feed into longer-term, global responses. This is the case in *Angels*, as it is in most play performances.

In general, spectators respond with longer-lasting and more intense emotions to narrative developments than they do to specific actor/characters. But spectators also form empathetic relationships with individual actor/characters as they watch their behaviors, and these relationships establish the basis for either 'sympathetic or antipathetic responses', according to Plantinga. That is, audiences take the well-being and goals of specific actor/characters as their object and respond to them with sympathy or with antipathy, its opposite. A major character set up for antipathetic response in *Angels* is Roy Cohn, whose Machiavellian cunning, obnoxious self-delusions, and murderous pursuit of victims to promote his own power, while often funny, easily type him as a villain. In *Perestroika*, Kushner establishes a conflict between Roy and Belise, a male nurse and former drag queen, who must care for Cohn, now afflicted with AIDS, as well as Prior, in a local hospital. Belise gets the better of Roy in their acerbic exchanges and finally steals some of his AIDS medication as he is dying. As audiences often do with antipathetic characters, spectators watching *Perestroika* enjoy laughing at actor/Roy and believe that his villainy partly justifies his suffering.

Kushner crafted Prior Walter as one of the most sympathetic characters in *Angels*, but the actor playing Harper Pitt, whose initial innocence and panic send her on hallucinogenic trips to Antarctica, will also gain some sympathy from most spectators in performance. Viewers who sympathize with actor/characters do not necessarily share in their experience of their own emotions. Spectators will probably appreciate actor/Prior's intelligence and wit and may experience some of his terror when he sees the Angel, but it is unlikely that they would want to put themselves through the pain he suffers from AIDS. Likewise, many spectators will feel sorry for actor/Harper's plight, but are unlikely to experience her panic with the same intensity that she does.

Of course, our response to actor/characters can change during the course of a performance; that is part of the fun of watching an emotionally complex play. Indeed, spectators may also come to believe that their response to an event in the narrative was mistaken and later reject their initial emotion for another one. We have all felt compassion for actor/ characters in difficult situations and later kicked ourselves, mentally, when we discovered that we had been duped by some artful faking. Plantinga calls such responses 'meta-emotions'; spectators respond in one way and then change their minds about their initial emotion and respond differently a second time. In *Perestroika*, Louis, having wrecked his relationship with Joe Pitt for progressive political reasons, asks Prior whether he can come back to him. Most people in the audience will probably feel contempt for Louis the first time he asks Prior to recommit to him. But he asks again a couple of minutes later and apologizes for having abandoned Prior. At that point, many spectators will likely feel his sincerity and loneliness and may regret their initial response of contempt. A larger reversal involving meta-emotion occurs earlier, when Roy Cohn dies. As he is weakening, Roy pleads for compassion from the ghost of Ethel Rosenberg, whom he sent to the electric chair through illegal means during the height of McCarthyism. She finally relents and sings him a Yiddish lullaby. Just when we think Roy has died, he sits up violently in bed and mocks Ethel for singing to him. Then, a moment later, the character really does die. Most in the audience, having been suckered into feeling a little compassion for the SOB during the lullaby, will abruptly reject that first response and rejoice in his death.

In addition to direct, global, sympathetic/antipathetic, and meta-emotions, Plantinga notes that performances often involve spectators in what he terms 'local' emotions. These are brief and intense, usually sparked by an effect that evokes surprise, disgust, or other kinds of shock. Both parts of *Angels* are full of them. Roy denies to his doctor that he is homosexual, an Eskimo appears in Harper's Antarctic hallucination, Louis Ironson kisses Joe Pitt, and an Angel busts through Prior's apartment ceiling. And that's just Part I. In retrospect, looking back from the end of the play, these and other startling effects are perfectly justified in terms of narrative development and the believability of the characters, but, in the moment of their occurrence, they have the effect of shock and awe. Horror movies, of course, thrive on such local emotions, and Kushner wants to grab his spectators and shake them up in many of the same ways.

All of the emotional responses discussed so far occur while spectators are experiencing the 'flow' of the fiction — while they are 'living in the blend', to use Fauconnier and Turner's terminology. As we have seen, however, audience members often step back from their involvement in the fictional action; they un-blend their actor/character integrations to enjoy performances in other ways. Plantinga calls these 'artifact' emotions, implicitly referring to the celluloid artifact that constitutes the material reality of a film. Examples of 'artifact' emotions in film viewing are the admiration a spectator may feel for the cameraman after watching a long and involved tracking shot or the response of disappointment in the realization that a normally good actor turned in a mediocre performance. While appropriate for film spectating, the term 'artifact emotion' does not translate well to live theatre. A better designation might be simply 'theatrical emotion', which implicitly distinguishes between the theatrical level of a production, involving actors, directors, playwrights, and so on, and the dramatic or fictional level, which (as we have seen) requires actor/characters interacting within a subjunctive world. Theatrical emotions could also include a spectator's emotional responses to the other auditors watching the production.

Regarding theatrical emotions in *Angels*, Kushner's script calls for the multiple casting of some actors, a convention on the theatrical level that was followed in all major professional productions during the 1990s. Multiple casting clearly impacted audience response. The 1996 printed version of *Perestroika*, for instance, indicates that the woman playing Hannah should also perform Ethel Rosenberg, one of the Angels in the Heaven scene, and four minor male characters in other scenes. In a crucial scene set in the Diorama Room of the Mormon Visitors Center in New York, the actor playing Joe Pitt should also play the Mormon Father in the animated diorama of wooden figures that depicts the Mormons' quest for a Promised Land in the American West. In these and other instances of multiple casting, the audience is invited to ask why the playwright and director decided to use the same actor for several roles. Audiences watching *Perestroika* will wonder what Hannah Pitt and Ethel Rosenberg have in common. They will ask why Joe Pitt and the Mormon Father are linked together. While several answers to these questions are possible, Kushner invites curious spectators to approach them through a main theme of his play, which is the gut-wrenching difficulty of genuine personal change. Both Hannah and Ethel faced enormous challenges in life (and Ethel continues to struggle after death to move past her bitterness). Yet, despite their difficulties, both transform themselves through the course of the action.

Joe Pitt, in contrast, remains much the same character he was at the start of *Millennium Approaches*. He is just as wooden in his beliefs and relationships as the mannequin in the Mormon diorama. And, like the mannequin, Joe remains stuck in the past, condemned to repeat his quest for religious perfection whenever anyone pushes a button to animate him. The double casting of the same actor for the mannequin as for the character of Joe invites the audience to compare two different blends: How is actor/Joe similar to actor/mannequin? For spectators, the body of the actor playing both roles provides the common concept, the anchor, onto which they can map the concepts of 'Joe' and 'Mormon Father mannequin'. Kushner's casting convention invites spectators to re-blend major actors with different, parallel characters. These new blends, shaped as well by the emotions behind them, will facilitate the emergence of new meanings for the audience regarding the initial actor/characters.

Memory and emotional contagion

A spectator's emotional engagements are always intertwined with memory. To use a printing metaphor, no spectator comes to the theatre as a blank piece of paper, devoid of memory, ready to receive all the impressions that a performance may print upon his or her mind. Older theatregoers bring with them memories of many previous productions, which may include knowledge of particular theatrical styles, recollections shaped by several dramatic genres, experiences in many theatrical venues, a familiarity with certain kinds of plots, and specific memories of actors, plays, scenic designs, and even lines of dialogue. And beyond memories that derive from theatregoing, playgoers will bring their personal histories and their entire culture with them into the auditorium. Although younger viewers carry less memorial baggage, the influence of parents, friends, and the media in their lives will also have molded their memories and shaped their expectations. Critics and historians can never hope to figure out all of the ties to memory that animate each spectator, of course, but scholars can work at the level of a play's relation to the general culture to speculate on the kinds of meanings that will probably emerge for most spectators during a performance. In *Angels*, for example, Prior's lines contain several references to popular films, from *The Wizard of Oz* to *Come Back, Little Sheba*. When the Angel crashes through his ceiling at the end of *Millennium*, Prior whispers, '*Very* Steven Spielberg' (p. 118). Kushner counts on the audience to understand most of Prior's references; their knowledge of popular culture helps spectators to build a sympathetic relationship with the actor/character during the performance.

Perhaps Kushner's most significant uses of cultural memory in *Angels* are the causal relationships he forges between the hysteria sparked by McCarthyism in the early 1950s and Reagan's presidency in the 1980s. Roy Cohn, Senator McCarthy's chief lawyer in the 1950s and an influence peddler with clout for Reagan's team in the 1980s, is the primary link. I have already noted that Kushner brings Ethel Rosenberg back from the dead to remind spectators of Cohn's worst crime during McCarthyism. She presides over his death rattles from AIDS and gloats when Cohn is disbarred just before his passing. During both plays, Roy angles to seduce Joe Pitt; he tries to move Joe into his bed and into Washington to work for the Justice Department. Willfully blind to Roy's manipulations, Joe never connects the dots to figure out that Cohn needs a 'butt boy' in DC in do his bidding at Justice. Nonetheless, Roy has placed him with an influential New York judge so that Joe can follow in his McCarthyite footsteps. As the judge's clerk, Joe writes what Louis terms 'an important bit of legal fag-bashing' (*Perestroika*, p. 109) that undercuts the right of homosexuals to equal protection under the law, rights they were also denied in the early 1950s. Then, at the climactic point of the scene that ends their affair, Louis demands of Joe, '*Have you no decency, at long last, sir, have you no decency at all'* (p. 109; italics in original). In his next speech, Louis shouts to Joe (which allows Kushner to explain to the audience) that he has just quoted the most famous line to come out of the Army–McCarthy Hearings, in which lawyer Joseph Welch finally condemned the Senator's (and Cohn's) 'fascist hypocrite lying filthy' tactics (p. 110). At the end of the scene, however, Joe is more worried about the fight he has just had with Louis than about the political consequences of his actions for the lives of thousands of homosexuals. Louis dismisses him with loathing, and most spectators, now fully aware of the dreadful ties between McCarthyism and Reaganism, will do the same. This meaning emerges through blending and memory. Spectators will blend actor/ Joe with their remembered concept of Senator McCarthy to link the two. Kushner evokes the cultural memories of McCarthyism to condemn similar political actions in the 1980s, especially the national administration's manipulation of ignorance, hypocrisy, and fear to deny full rights to the LGBT (lesbian, gay, bisexual, and transgendered) community and to prolong the AIDS epidemic.

I have been discussing the emotions of individual spectators, but it is clear that many emotional responses, especially those that engage general cultural memory, will sweep across most of an audience. Psychologists call this 'emotional contagion' and it is common in the theatre. We evolved from creatures that traveled in groups, and the need for solidarity forged through emotional contagion to enable everyday cooperation and defense against predators remains

a strong part of our evolutionary heritage. Emotional contagion in the playhouse, usually sparked by a stimulus from
the stage and the millisecond triggering of mirror neurons
in many spectator brains interacting together, is automatic
and usually very quick. Audiences will tend to laugh, cry,
and even gasp simultaneously. Most of the types of emotional responses we have been discussing – direct, global,
sympathetic/antipathetic, meta-emotion, and theatrical
emotion – will travel among many, if not all, auditors at different levels of intensity and duration during a performance.
Local responses – the quick shocks of surprise, disgust, or
other primary emotions – will jolt nearly everyone in an
auditorium.

'Emotional entrainment', an extreme form of contagion,
will involve almost all spectators in its driving rhythms.
Entrainment occurs most frequently in musical performances. According to musicologist Michael Thaut,

> Several key findings in rhythmic synchroniza-
> tion research have emerged that contribute to
> an understanding of the neurobiological basis of
> music and temporal information processing in
> the brain. Musical rhythm rapidly creates sta-
> ble and precise internal templates for temporal
> organization of motor responses. The motor
> system is very sensitive to the auditory system.
> Neural impulses of auditory rhythm project
> directly onto motor structures. Motor responses
> become entrained to the timing of rhythmic

patterns. ('Rhythm, Human Temporality, and Brain Function', 2005, p. 184)

A song in a musical comedy or, even more so, a kick-line of dancers stepping to the same tune will lock in audience motor responses at the neurological level. The cognitive dynamics of mirror neurons firing in synchrony are the same as other forms of emotional contagion, but the emotional response to entrainment is often more intense and longer lasting. Spectators can resist entrainment, just as they can resist other emotional engagements. Most auditors, however, enjoy the feelings of togetherness that emotional contagion and entrainment entail. Although theatre audiences are generally less rowdy than spectators at sports games and rock concerts, they, too, often want to be moved by the same group emotions.

Performative networks

People at the theatre respond as individuals, as an entire audience, and also as a part of a larger network. All theatrical productions occur within performance networks, webs of connected performers, spectators, and others who have an interest (aesthetic, economic, emotional, ideological, etc.) in the ongoing success and continuation of particular kinds of performances. Like social networks shared among computer and cell phone users, some performance networks are broad and inclusive, drawing in thousands of spectators, theatre artists, marketing professionals, and others whose business is not solely connected to show biz, such as printers and fabric manufacturers. Other networks are comparatively narrow — a ring of classmates, friends, faculty, parents, and others for a student theatrical production at a university, for example. Whatever their size, networks are relatively stable groupings of similar kinds of people, with varying dynamics of inclusion and exclusion, that constrain and enable sociality, identity construction, and other social practices before, during, and after a performance. Networks are sociological categories, useful for grouping average beliefs and responses but not reliable for determining individual actions. Nonetheless, because we are social animals, we tend to respond within the boundaries of our networks; it is generally more enjoyable to laugh, grow sad, and feel outrage with other people at the theatre who share our beliefs and values. Responding alone, like bowling alone, can be isolating.

All performance networks, for live as well as mediated productions, limit the reach of every drama, including the kinds of meanings that spectators within a network will tend to generate. In this sense, performance networks are also performative networks; they enable and constrain the networking of our neurons and the meanings we make through them, through our bodies, and through our ecology. Even though there is a huge international network for Hollywood films, US producers regularly adjust their movies for sub-networks within their total network. They know that certain films will appeal to specific demographics around the world and that those audiences will be able to make many enjoyable meanings from them. The producers cast, shoot, and market their products accordingly. Hollywood released Michael Almereyda's *Hamlet* in 2000, staring Ethan Hawke in the lead and Sam Shepard as the Ghost of Hamlet's father. Almereyda updated his version of *Hamlet* to the late twentieth century, figuring the old king as the CEO of a corporation and Hamlet as his disaffected son, no longer a prince away at school but a Gen X videographer.

Many movie viewers around the world would have recognized Hawke, but the casting of Shepard, and the possible meanings that might have emerged for viewers from his playing of the Ghost, were probably specific to one subnetwork within global Hollywood. Shepard/Ghost appears in a long leather trench coat smoking a cigarette, an image meant to evoke television commercials from the 1960s and 1970s featuring the Marlboro man. In his few film roles, including Chuck Yeager in *The Right Stuff* (1983), Shepard usually played such a figure – a lone cowboy embodying individualistic, frontier values. Further, some film viewers would have known that Shepard was also a playwright; his 1970s dramas, such as the Pulitzer Prize–winning *Buried Child*, are still celebrated for their penetrating insights into American masculinity and dysfunctional family life. By 2000, when Almereyda's *Hamlet* premiered, however, Shepard had apparently given up writing difficult plays for small audiences. In short, as cognitive critic Amy Cook notes, 'As the ghost of Hamlet's father, Shepard is the death of theater. ... He is crying for revenge to a son who we know will only disappoint him. He is the old west and high art looking to a disaffected New York arty intellectual for

71

salvation. He is the past left homeless by the apathetic, post-modern present' (*Shakespearean Neuroplay*, 2010, p. 112).

But Shepard as the Ghost in Almereyda's *Hamlet* could resonate with these meanings only for people who traveled in a specific sub-network of global Hollywood. As Cook knows, Shepard/Ghost could not be the 'death of theater' for people who did not know that Shepard wrote 'high art' plays. He could not be the image of the 'old west' for those who never saw a Marlboro cigarette commercial. And he could not be the hero with the 'right stuff' for those who never saw him play Chuck Yeager and similar characters. The demographic that might have been able to perceive these meanings in Shepard's Ghost when the film was released was probably an English-speaking US citizen over forty who had a history of attending challenging films and also possessed a knowledge of the American theatre. For spectators to see the 'death of theater', the 'old west', and the 'right stuff' in Shepard/Ghost, they had to be able to make those blends. This means that they had to recollect mental concepts for those three qualities before they could blend them with Shepard and relate them to the possible meanings of his Ghost in the film. Others who were not US citizens over forty and lacked the typical background of that network may also have had concepts for these three qualities, but the chances that they remembered all of them are slim; networks generally get constructed through common cultural experiences. The sub-network for whom these meanings likely emerged in 2000 could have been only a small slice of *Hamlet's* international audience.

It is important to emphasize that the film of *Hamlet* in 2000, or any play in any medium of performance, does not 'contain' the meanings that audience members might attribute to it. Almereyda's *Hamlet* required cognitive construction from the audience before the meanings of Shepard/Ghost could emerge for them; in addition to their general cognitive capabilities for spectating, their memory and blending really got a workout. Likewise, Kushner's *Angels* provided viewers in the 1990s with the possibility of perceiving his broadly democratic and socialist themes through its images, dialogue, and emotions – but only the possibility. The meanings of any performance always emerge from the interplay among performers, spectators, and the other agents in the network. Performances are not one-way delivery systems shoveling content and meaning from artists to audiences. In a strict sense, performances by themselves present no ready-made meanings at all. In their interactions with embodied spectators located in specific networks, though, performances may energize people to make hundreds, even thousands, of blends and meanings.

This is as true for critics, theorists, and historians as it is for regular spectators. Even those theorists who seek to deny the importance of evolution and cognition for understanding the theatre cannot help but perceive initial meanings through the same foundational cognitive operations as everybody else. As for theatre historians, their investigations depend on their ability to empathize with past actors and spectators who possessed all of the same foundational capabilities that animate actors and spectators today. As we have seen, engagement with and meaning-making in the theatre depend upon the neurological actions of perception, blending, and ecology. Society and culture are important as well, of course, because without a social network that enables, shapes, and constrains possible meanings, no performative communication is possible. Consequently, different networks always afford different possibilities for meaning. Much the same could be said for theorists and historians of performance. Without a discursive network of committed authors and readers, no cultural communication about our mutual fascination with the theatre is possible. And because networks always afford different possibilities for meaning, I believe it is time for us to put aside past prejudices and paradigms to investigate together the evolutionary and cognitive foundations of performance.

further reading

The published works below are primarily of three kinds. You will find some that focus specifically on applying relevant insights from the cognitive sciences to theatre and performance studies. Many more, however, are intended for general readers interested in various aspects of evolution and cognition. Finally, I have included a few theatrical books, plays, and articles that I cited in my text because they were relevant to my argument, even though they were written before the cognitive revolution.

Barrett, Lisa, Paula Niedenthal, and Piotr Winkielman, eds. *Emotion and Consciousness*. New York: Guilford Press, 2005.

Blair, Rhonda. *The Actor, Image, and Action: Acting and Cognitive Neuroscience*. New York: Routledge, 2008.

Boyd, Brian. *On the Origin of Stories: Evolution, Cognition, and Fiction*. Cambridge, MA: Harvard UP, 2009.

Chekhov, Michael. *To the Actor*. New York: Harper & Row, 1985.

———. *The Path of the Actor*. Ed. Andrei Kirillov and Bella Merlin. New York: Routledge, 2005.

Cook, Amy. *Shakespearean Neuroplay: Reinvigorating the Study of Dramatic Texts and Performance through Cognitive Science.* New York: Palgrave Macmillan, 2010.

Crane, Mary Thomas. *Shakespeare's Brain: Reading with Cognitive Theory.* Princeton, NJ: Princeton UP, 2001.

Damasio, Antonio. *The Feeling of What Happens: Body and Emotion in the Making of Consciousness.* New York: Harcourt Brace, 1999.

————. *Looking for Spinoza: Joy, Sorrow, and the Feeling Brain.* New York: Harcourt Brace, 2003.

Doidge, Norman. *The Brain That Changes Itself.* New York: Penguin, 2007.

Donald, Merlin. *A Mind So Rare: The Evolution of Human Consciousness.* New York: W.W. Norton, 2001.

Edelman, Gerald M. *Second Nature: Brain Science and Human Knowledge.* New Haven, CT: Yale UP, 2006.

Edelman, Gerald M., and Giulio Tononi. *A Universe of Consciousness: How Matter Becomes Imagination.* New York: Basic Books, 2000.

Ekman, Paul. *Emotions Revealed: Recognizing Faces and Feelings to Improve Communication and Emotional Life.* New York: Henry Holt, 2003.

Eversmann, Peter. 'The Experience of the Theatrical Event.' *Theatrical Events: Borders, Dynamics, Frames.* Ed. Vicki Ann Cremona, Peter Eversmann, Hans van Maanen, Willmar Sauter, and John Tulloch. Amsterdam and New York: Rodopi, 2004. 139–74.

Fauconnier, Gilles, and Mark Turner. *The Way We Think: Conceptual Blending and the Mind's Hidden Complexity.* New York: Basic Books, 2002.

Fletcher, Angus. *Evolving Hamlet: Seventeenth-Century English Tragedy and the Ethics of Natural Selection.* New York: Palgrave Macmillan, 2011.

Gallagher, Shaun, and Dan Zahavi. *The Phenomenological Mind: An Introduction to Philosophy of Mind and Cognitive Science.* New York: Routledge, 2008.

Gibson, James J. *The Ecological Approach to Visual Perception.* Boston: Houghton Mifflin, 1979.

Johnson, Mark. *The Meaning of the Body: Aesthetics of Human Understanding.* Chicago: U of Chicago P, 2007.

Kemp, Richard J. 'Embodied Acting: Cognitive Foundations of Performance.' PhD Diss. University of Pittsburgh, 2010.

Kushner, Tony. *Angels in America: Millennium Approaches*. New York: TCG, 1993.

———. *Angels in America: Perestroika*. New York, TCG, 1996.

Lakoff, George, and Mark Johnson. *Philosophy in the Flesh: The Embodied Mind and Its Challenge to Western Thought*. New York: Basic Books, 1999.

Lecoq, Jacques. *The Moving Body*. Trans. David Bradby. New York: Routledge, 2001.

Lutterbie, John. *Toward a General Theory of Acting*. New York: Palgrave Macmillan, 2011.

McConachie, Bruce. *Engaging Audiences: A Cognitive Approach to Spectating in the Theatre*. New York: Palgrave Macmillan, 2008.

———. 'Moving Spectators toward Progressive Politics by Combining Brechtian Theory with Cognitive Science.' *Playing with Theory in Theatre Practice*. Ed. Megan Alrutz, Julia Listengarten, and M. Van Duyn Wood. New York: Palgrave Macmillan, 2012. 148–60.

———. 'Reenacting Events to Narrate Theatre History.' *Representing the Past: Essays in Performance Historiography*. Ed. Charlotte Canning and Thomas Postlewait. Iowa City: U of Iowa P, 2010. 378–403.

McConachie, Bruce, and F. Elizabeth Hart, eds. *Performance and Cognition: Theatre Studies and the Cognitive Turn*. New York: Routledge, 2006.

McNeill, David. *Gesture and Thought*. Chicago: U of Chicago P, 2005.

———. *Language and Gesture*. Cambridge: Cambridge UP, 2000.

Müller, Heiner. *Hamletmachine and Other Texts for the Stage*. Ed. and trans. Carl Weber. New York: PAJ, 1984.

Nalbantian, Suzanne, Paul M. Matthews, and James L. McClelland, eds. *The Memory Process*. Cambridge, MA: MIT Press, 2011.

Paavolainen, Teemu. *Theatre / Ecology / Cognition: Theorizing Performer-Object Interaction in Grotowski, Kantor, and Meyerhold*. Tampere, Finland: Tampere UP, 2011.

Panksepp, Jaak. *Affective Neuroscience: The Foundations of Human and Animal Emotions*, New York: Oxford UP, 1998.

Plantinga, Carl. *Moving Viewers: American Film and the Spectator's Experience*. Berkeley and London: U of California P, 2009.

Robbins, Philip, and Murat Aydede, eds. *The Cambridge Handbook of Situated Cognition*. New York: Cambridge UP, 2009.

Rokotnitz, Naomi. *Trusting Performance: A Cognitive Approach to Embodiment in Drama*. New York: Palgrave Macmillan, 2011.

Schechner, Richard. *Performance Studies: An Introduction*. 2nd edn. New York: Routledge, 2006.

Semin, Gun, and Eliot Smith, eds. *Embodied Grounding: Social, Cognitive, Affective, and Neuroscientific Approaches*. Cambridge: Cambridge UP, 2008.

Sheets-Johnstone, Maxine. *The Primacy of Movement*. Amsterdam: John Benjamins, 1999.

Smith, Anna Deavere. *Fires in the Mirror: Crown Heights, Brooklyn, and Other Identities*. New York: Doubleday, 1993.

Stewart, John, Olivier Gapenne, and Ezequiel A. DiPaola, eds. *Enaction: Toward a New Paradigm for Cognitive Science*. Cambridge, MA: MIT Press, 2010.

Stromberg, Peter G. *Caught in Play: How Entertainment Works on You*. Stanford, CA: Stanford UP, 2009.

Sutton-Smith, Brian. *The Ambiguity of Play*. Cambridge, MA: Harvard UP, 1997.

Thaut, Michael H. 'Rhythm, Human Temporality, and Brain Function.' *Musical Communication*. Ed. Dorothy Miell, Raymond MacDonald, and Donald J. Hargreaves. Oxford: Oxford UP, 2005. 171–91.

Thompson, Evan. *Mind in Life: Biology, Phenomenology, and the Sciences of Mind*. Cambridge, MA: Harvard UP, 2007.

Tribble, Evelyn B. *Cognition in the Globe: Attention and Memory in Shakespeare's Theatre*. New York: Palgrave Macmillan, 2011.

Turner, Mark, ed. *The Artful Mind: Cognitive Science and the Riddle of Human Creativity*. New York: Oxford UP, 2006.

Wexler, Bruce E. *Brain and Culture: Neurobiology, Ideology, and Social Change*. Cambridge, MA: MIT Press, 2006.

Zunshine, Lisa. *Introduction to Cognitive Cultural Studies*. Baltimore, MD: Johns Hopkins UP, 2010.

index